SCHOLASTIC

VOCABULARY-BUILDING Card Games

GRADE 2

BY LIANE B. ONISH

NEW YORK • TORONTO • LONDON • AUCKLAND • SYDNEY
MEXICO CITY • NEW DELHI • HONG KONG • BUENOS AIRES

Teaching
Resources

Hi, Mom!

Editor: Joan Novelli
Cover design by Maria Lilja.
Interior design by Kathy Massaro.
Interior art by Anne Kennedy.

ISBN 13: 978-0-439-55465-7
ISBN 10: 0-439-55465-9

Contents

About This Book

Vocabulary games make words fun to learn and easier to remember, and they strengthen reading and literacy skills. The more words children can recognize easily, the more they will read; and the more children read, the more words they will know, which will make them better and more willing readers, and stronger speakers, spellers, writers, and test takers.

This book features 20 engaging, easy-to-make, easy-to-play card games and dozens of variations to help students learn more than 300 words and develop and reinforce valuable vocabulary skills. Research shows that vocabulary development is highly correlated with overall student success. "Having a strong vocabulary is of particular importance to students in that it contributes significantly to achievement both in the subjects of their school curriculum and also on standardized tests" (Shostak, 2002). Direct instruction and reading widely are both important factors in increasing students' vocabulary. Repeated exposure to words and independent practice with them are also essential, and word games are an effective way to provide these opportunities.

The 300-plus words featured in these vocabulary games, all key additions to children's growing vocabularies, were selected from a variety of sources.

✳ 150 most frequent words list: These high-frequency, nondecodable words are essential to reading, writing, and comprehension and make up about half of all printed materials. (*American Heritage Word Frequency Book*; as cited in Blevins, 2006)

✳ Dolch Basic Sight Vocabulary 220 list: These words represent a large percentage of those that readers will encounter in textbooks, and are necessary for reading fluency.

✳ Fry's 300 Instant Sight Words: Divided into groups of 100 that approximately correlate with grade-level vocabulary, these are among the most common words used in reading and writing. (Fry & Kress, 2006)

✳ Environmental print and grade-level literature

Designed to provide both the playful approach and repeated practice that support effective learning, the games in this book and their many variations can be played again and again to build and deepen word knowledge, strengthen related skills, and make the learning stick.

How Much Practice?

"How much practice is the right amount? . . . It is difficult to overstate the value of practice. For a new skill to become automatic or for new knowledge to become long-lasting, sustained practice, *beyond the point of mastery*, is necessary" (Willingham, 2004). Research shows that we need about 12 encounters with, or exposures to, a new word before we know it well enough to comprehend it in text (Beck, McKeown, & Kucan, 2002). Enough encounters with a word and it will find its way into our oral and written vocabularies. Vocabulary games, as a regular part of classroom life, can give children the multiple encounters they need to "own" more words.

What's Inside?

In addition to 20 word games, you'll find extra game cards and blank game card templates for customizing games, and a master list of target words for easy reference and for fluency practice. Here's a closer look at each section of the book.

Pages 9–11: Master Word List

An alphabetical list of all the words is included for reference. You can use this list to create speed drill practice for reading fluency and automaticity. (See More Ways to Use the Word Cards, page 7.)

Pages 12–71: Vocabulary Games

Directions for 20 vocabulary-building games follow a simple format to make it easy for students to set up and play.

※ **Skill:** All games are designed to build vocabulary. Some games may have additional areas of instructional focus, such as recognizing parts of speech.

※ **Number of Players:** Games provide opportunities for varied groupings, from one or two students to the entire class.

※ **Object of the Game:** How to win varies from game to game.

※ **Materials:** In addition to game cards, this section lists any other materials students need to play, such as a timer, crayons, or index cards.

※ **How to Play:** Step-by-step directions make it easy to set up and get started.

※ **More Ways to Play:** Suggestions in this section help teachers create simpler or more challenging games to meet the learning needs of different groups of students.

What the Research Says

"Intuition tells us that more practice leads to better memory. Research tells us something more precise: Memory in either the short- or long-term requires ongoing practice."

(Willingham, 2004)

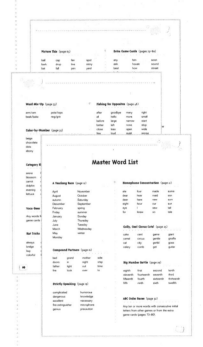

Teaching Tip

You'll find that many of the games work with cards from other games as well as with the extra cards (pages 73–80). You can also adapt the games for use with specific content area vocabulary. Simply copy the blank game card templates (page 72), and write in desired words. Review the game directions with those words in mind, and make any adjustments that might be necessary.

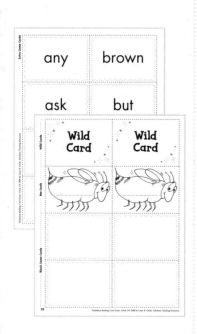

Each game focuses on a particular set of words. These may be sight words, number words, compound words, words that represent parts of speech, and so on. For some games, such as Word-O! (page 67), you will select game cards as you wish from other games or from the extra cards provided (pages 73–80). Or you may use the blank game card templates (page 72) to create your own, using content vocabulary, books children are reading, or other classroom sources of vocabulary. For other games, such as Category Slap-Down (page 39), target words are specified and game cards are provided accordingly. However, for any of the games, you can use the extra game cards and blank game card templates to customize vocabulary.

Pages 72–80: Extra Game Cards

These pages feature extra game cards for use with specific games, as well as for use in customizing any game. The Wild Cards (page 72) are for use with Homophone Concentration (page 21), but you may also find these useful to create variations on other games. The Bee Cards (page 72), used with Voca-Bees (page 43), can also serve as playful game card templates for any game in which you are creating word cards. Blank game card templates (pages 72) are also provided for this purpose. In addition, there are 64 extra word cards (pages 73–80), useful for games that specify "any word cards," and to create customized word card sets for other games.

Teaching With the Games

You can use the games in any order that best supports your teaching needs. Following are suggestions for teaching with the games—from setup and storage to helping players decide who goes first.

Setup and Storage

Once you choose a game and gather any necessary materials, it's worth the effort to take a few minutes to set up a storage system. With the setup that follows, students can easily use the games at school as well as transport them home to play with families, reinforcing the connections between home and school that lead to more successful learning.

1. For durability, photocopy the game cards on cardstock, or glue to index cards and laminate.

2. Clip the cards for each game together (or place them in an envelope) and store in a resealable plastic bag. Consider making a second set of cards for each game as backup. (Place these in an envelope and label "Extra Set of Cards.")

3. Label each bag with the name of the game, the skill it reinforces, and the number of players.

4. Photocopy the directions and tape them to the inside of the bag.

Teaching Tip

The Contents page summarizes specific skills to assist with choosing a game that provides practice in a desired area.

Introducing the Games

Introduce the games one at a time in any order that best matches your language arts program and your students' needs. Model how to play, including for individual players, pairs, small groups, and the whole class. (See Number of Players for each game.) Keep in mind that the games provide support for differentiated learning. Each game includes suggestions for variations, including, for example, using fewer or more word cards and simplifying or increasing the level of vocabulary difficulty. You may also choose games to use with students based on an identified need. Students who need additional practice with writing and reading words for the months of the year, for example, will benefit from playing A Yearlong Race (page 12). Homophone Concentration (page 21) is just right for students who need practice with easily confused words.

Who Goes First?

There are many ways to decide who goes first in a game. Here are a few ideas from which students can choose:

❉ Use a set of alphabet cards. Have each player pick a card. The player whose word is closest to *A* (or *Z*) goes first. The player with the next closest letter goes second, and so on.

❉ Use children's first, last, or middle initials to determine order of play.

❉ Have players roll a die. The player who rolls the highest number goes first. The next player is the one sitting to the left of the first player. For variety, have the player who rolls the lowest number go first.

❉ Mix up the word cards for the game. Deal one card to each player. The player whose word is closest to *A* (or *Z*) goes first.

Teaching Tip

As students revisit games and words, encourage them to use prior knowledge to make new connections. Is there a synonym, antonym, or homonym they know? Can they give a definition or use the word in context? When they come to an unknown word, encourage them to look for part of the word that looks familiar. How can they use what they know about word parts to understand an unfamiliar word?

Bibliography

Beck, I. L., McKeown, M. G., & Kucan, L. (2002). *Bringing Words to Life: Robust Vocabulary Instruction.* New York: The Guilford Press.

Blevins, W. (2006). *Phonics From A to Z: A Practical Guide* (2nd ed.). New York: Scholastic.

Fry, E. B., & Kress, J. E. (2006). *The Reading Teacher's Book of Lists* (5th ed.). San Francisco, CA: Jossey-Bass.

Kamil, M. L., Mosenthal, P. B., Pearson, P. D., & Barr, R. (Eds.). (2000). *Handbook of Reading Research, Vol. III.* Mahwah, NJ: Lawrence Erlbaum Associates.

Shostak, J. (2002). "The Value of Direct and Systematic Vocabulary Instruction." Retrieved September 27, 2007, from www.sadlier-oxford.com/docs/pdf/9147-9_VW_WhitePaper_Vol7.pdf.

Willingham, D. T. (2004, Spring). "Practice Makes Perfect—But Only if You Practice Beyond the Point of Perfection." *American Educator.*

More Ways to Use the Word Cards

In addition to using the word cards to play the games in this book, there are many other ways you can use them to provide the practice children need to achieve long-lasting learning. Following are some suggestions.

✳ **Word Basket:** Make a set of word cards and keep them in a large basket or box. Grab handfuls to use as flash cards. Distribute one word to each child for lineup. Have children arrange themselves in alphabetical order according to the word on their cards. Then collect the cards when everyone is in line, reading them together as you go.

✳ **My Words!** Give children a bag or box to use for their personal game cards and other vocabulary words. Let children add words from books, phonics practice pages, and spelling lessons. Periodically, have them select a few at random to use in oral and written stories, sorting games, and alphabetizing activities.

✳ **Collectors:** Give children a blank word card (page 72) to use as a bookmark for their daily independent reading. Let them choose a word from their reading to share with a book group. Have them write the word on the card and draw a picture or use it in a sentence on the back. After sharing their words, children can add them to their My Words! collection.

✳ **Fluency Practice:** Use the word cards as a resource for fluency practice. Select a handful of cards at random, alphabetically from the master list (pages 9–11), or with similar/confusing phonetic elements. Write the words on a 30-, 40-, or 50-word grid (5 x 6, 5 x 8, or 5 x 10), and duplicate for each child. Let children practice reading the words until they are ready to be timed.

A Note About Word Parts

Learning to break longer words into smaller, recognizable parts is an essential tool for vocabulary development. Of new words a student encounters in reading, approximately 60 percent can be analyzed into parts that provide significant help in determining meaning. (Nagy & Anderson, 1984; as cited in Kamil, Mosenthal, Pearson, & Barr; 2000) A study of Greek and Latin roots helps students build knowledge of word parts. Greek and Latin were influential languages, and they contributed roots for many everyday words to other languages. For example, the Greek word *teckhne* meant "something made by human intelligence," and it forms the root of our words *technical* and *technique.*

You can build students' base for comprehension by looking for opportunities as they play the games in this book to point out and teach common Greek and Latin roots. For example, with Category Slap-Down (page 39), take time to investigate the word *octopus* (Greek: *okto* meaning "eight" and *pous* meaning "foot"). Encourage students to use what they know about these word parts to figure out the meaning of other words they encounter, such as *octopod* and *octagon.*

Master Word List

A Yearlong Race (page 12)

April	November
August	October
autumn	Saturday
December	September
February	spring
Friday	summer
January	Sunday
July	Thursday
June	Tuesday
March	Wednesday
May	winter
Monday	

Compound Partners (page 16)

bed	grand	mother	side
doors	in	night	step
father	light	out	time
fire	look	over	to

Strictly Speaking (page 19)

complicated	humorous
dangerous	knowledge
excellent	necessary
fire extinguisher	microphone
genius	precaution

Homophone Concentration (page 21)

ate	four	made	some
dear	hear	maid	son
deer	here	new	sum
eight	hour	our	sun
eye	I	sew	tail
for	knew	so	tale

Golly, Gee! Circus Cats! (page 25)

cake	cent	game	giant
camel	circus	gentle	giraffe
cat	city	gerbil	goes
celery	comb	get	guitar

Big Number Battle (page 29)

eighth	first	second	tenth
eleventh	fourteenth	seventh	third
fifteenth	fourth	sixteenth	thirteenth
fifth	ninth	sixth	twelfth

ABC Order Races (page 32)

Any ten or more words with consecutive initial letters from other games or from the extra game cards (pages 73–80).

Word Mix-Up (page 33)

arm/ram	pots/tops
beak/bake	ring/grin

Color-by-Number (page 35)

beige	lavender	peach	turquoise
chocolate	lime	ruby	violet
dots	magenta	swirls	wavy
ebony	olive	teal	zigzag

Category Slap-Down (page 39)

arena	lobster	pigeon	store
blossom	midnight	robin	theater
carrot	morning	school	tomato
dolphin	noon	shark	tree
evening	octopus	shrub	turkey
lettuce	ostrich	spinach	weed

Voca-Bees (page 43)

Any words from other games or from the extra game cards (pages 73–80).

Hat Tricks (page 44)

always	cook	help	she
bridge	country	I	them
buy	early	month	under
colorful	he	pull	village

Fishing for Opposites (page 48)

after	goodbye	many	right
all	hello	more	small
before	large	narrow	start
better	left	none	stop
close	less	open	wide
few	loud	quiet	worse

Face It (page 52)

anger	giggle	scream	weep
fear	goofy	surprise	worry

Transportation Mix-Up (page 55)

ambulance	monorail
automobile	subway
bicycle	tractor
fire engine	unicycle

Now and Then (page 59)

blew	drank	said	sting
blow	drink	sang	stung
came	keep	say	take
catch	kept	sing	took
caught	lend	sleep	write
come	lent	slept	wrote

Picture This (page 63)

ball	cap	fan	spot
bark	drop	line	story
bat	fall	pen	yard

Bits and Pieces (page 65)

banjo	equal	hanger	slipper
chicken	finger	pocket	turtle

Word-O! (page 67)

Any 12 words from other games or from the extra game cards (pages 73–80).

What Went Where? (page 69)

wear	whale	which	woman
week	what	while	women
welcome	when	white	wonder
went	where	why	wool

Extra Game Cards (pages 73–80)

any	him	soon
ask	house	sound
best	how	street
both	into	sure
brown	just	teacher
but	know	thank
candle	now	their
child	once	then
children	pair	thermos
cold	party	tower
crawl	please	town
desk	police	twin
dinosaur	pretty	upset
doctor	purple	us
dresser	puzzle	volcano
end	quiz	wait
every	read	wheelchair
fence	remember	would
follow	sandwich	year
funny	short	zip
gift	should	
hers	snake	

A Yearlong Race

Skill: Identifying months and days in order

Number of Players: 1 or 2, or teams (of no more than 12 players each)

Object of the Game: To arrange months of the year and days of the week in order

Materials

❋ game cards (pages 13–15)

❋ timer

❋ tables or whiteboard trays (for teams)

Getting Ready

Photocopy and cut out game cards for the names of the months, days of the week, and seasons. Note that for the seasons game cards, *autumn* is used. If you prefer, use the blank card (page 15) to change this to *fall* in advance of playing.

How to Play

One Player:

1. Mix up a set of month cards. Set a timer.

2. The player arranges the months in order from January through December.

3. When all the cards are in the correct order, the player notes the time on a sheet of paper and labels it "Round 1."

4. The player repeats steps 1–3 several times to try to better his or her score (labeling each time accordingly).

5. Repeat with days of the week, followed by seasons.

Teams:

1. Mix up a set of month cards and stack facedown in front of each team. Teams line up some distance from their playing field (a table or whiteboard tray).

2. The first player on each team takes the top card and runs to the team's playing field. The player places the card about where it should go in order. For example, the word card *February* should be placed on the left of the playing field, the word card *November* just right of the center. The player runs to the back of the line.

3. Each team player adds one card to the playing field and rearranges the cards that are there as needed.

4. The winner is the first team to place the months in the correct order.

5. Repeat with days of the week, followed by seasons.

More Ways to Play

❋ **From Now 'Til Next Year:** Use game cards for the months of the year, but instead of beginning with January, have players begin with the current month.

❋ **All Week, All Year, Four Seasons:** Add the game cards for the seasons. Have players arrange the game cards for the months of the year, placing the season cards next to the months in which each season begins.

January

May

February

June

March

July

April

August

September

Sunday

October

Monday

November

Tuesday

December

Wednesday

Vocabulary-Building Card Games: Grade 2 © 2008 by Liane B. Onish, Scholastic Teaching Resources

Thursday	spring
Friday	summer
Saturday	autumn
winter	

Compound Partners

grand

step

Skill: Recognizing compound words

Number of Players: Pairs

Object of the Game: To build compound words by putting words together

Materials

❄ game cards (pages 17–18)

❄ timer (optional)

Getting Ready

Photocopy and cut apart a set of game cards for each pair of players. Have available paper and pencils available.

How to Play

1. Review compound words: new words made by putting two smaller words together. Remind children that sometimes they can figure out the meaning of a compound word by looking at the meanings of the small words—for example, *homework* is work done at home. However, *butterfly* is not a stick of butter with wings.

2. Set a timer for five minutes (optional). When you say "Go," have pairs use the word cards to build compound words. Tell players they can use the small words more than once. Players list the compound words they make on paper.

3. The winner is the pair with the most compound words.

More Ways to Play

❄ **Compound Definitions:** Have players write definitions for the compound words they make. Then have them use the dictionary to check their definitions.

❄ **Mix and Match:** Play with the whole group. Give each child a game card (one half of a compound word). (Use the blank game cards on page 72 to make extra cards as needed.) Have children mingle, looking for someone who has a word card that makes a compound word with theirs. Players can join with two other players if they can mix and match their words to make two or more compound words—for example, children with the game cards *in, side,* and *to* can join together to make *inside* and *into*.

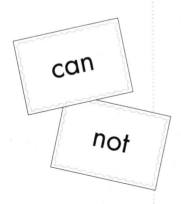

bed

grand

doors

in

fire

light

Vocabulary-Building Card Games: Grade 2 © 2008 by Liane B. Onish, Scholastic Teaching Resources

father

look

mother	side
night	step
out	time
over	to

Vocabulary-Building Card Games: Grade 2 © 2008 by Liane B. Onish, Scholastic Teaching Resources

Strictly Speaking

Skill: Building oral vocabulary

Number of Players: Teams of 2 or 3

Object of the Game: To collect the most word cards

How to Play

1. Have players in each group sit together.

2. Read each word and its context sentence. Have players on each team discuss the meaning of the word and stand up when they think they know it.

3. The first team to correctly tell what the word means collects the game card.

4. The team with the most cards at the end of the game wins.

More Ways to Play

❋ **Subject-ively Speaking:** Create a set of game cards using words from content areas, seasonal topics, or books you are reading aloud.

❋ **Dictionary:** Play as above, but after reading the context sentence, provide either a correct or incorrect definition for the word. Players decide if the definition is correct or not. If incorrect, they must tell what they think the word means.

Materials

❋ game cards (page 20)

❋ extra game cards (pages 73–80; optional)

❋ blank game card templates (page 72; optional)

Getting Ready

Photocopy and cut apart (or create) a set of ten game cards. These cards have both a word and a context sentence on them. You may use the prepared game cards if the target vocabulary words are in children's listening and oral vocabularies and above their reading level. Otherwise, substitute appropriate word cards from other games in this book or from the extra game cards (pages 73–80), and write a context sentence on each. You may also use the blank game card templates (page 72) to create your own set of game cards. Write both a word and context sentence on each card, for a total of ten game cards. Again, whether using the prepared cards or creating your own set, choose words that are in children's listening and oral vocabularies and above their reading level.

complicated

The pattern was too **complicated** for beginners to follow.

humorous

She read a **humorous** story and everyone laughed.

dangerous

It is **dangerous** to sail without wearing a life jacket.

knowledge

Their **knowledge** of the subject made the report interesting.

excellent

We applauded the **excellent** performance by the actors.

microphone

The **microphone** helped everyone hear the speaker.

fire extinguisher

They used the **fire extinguisher** to put out the flames.

necessary

It was **necessary** to stay indoors because of the storm.

genius

The **genius** solved the problem that no one else could figure out.

precaution

As a **precaution**, we took umbrellas with us.

Vocabulary-Building Card Games: Grade 2 © 2008 by Liane B. Onish, Scholastic Teaching Resources

Homophone Concentration

Skill: Matching words that sound the same but have different spellings and meanings

Number of Players: 2

Object of the Game: To collect the most sets of word cards

How to Play

1. Review the words with players.

2. Mix up the cards (word cards and Wild Cards together) and arrange them facedown in a rectangular array.

3. Play as you would play Concentration. The first player turns over two cards. If the cards show a pair of homophones, the player must use each word in a sentence before taking the pair of cards. Then the player turns over two more cards. If the two cards do not match, the player turns them facedown and the next player takes a turn.

4. If a player turns over a Wild Card, the player may write a word on it to make a pair.

5. If a player turns over two Wild Cards, the player may write any pair of homophones on the cards to make a match.

6. The winner is the player with the most word sets.

Materials

※ game cards (pages 22–24)

※ Wild Cards (page 72)

Getting Ready

Photocopy and cut apart the game cards and two Wild Cards.

More Ways to Play

※ **Word-Word-Word Concentration:** Use "triplets" to create a new game, or add them to the original game (above): *to, too, two*; *their, there, they're*; *cent, sent, scent*; *aisle, I'll, isle*; *do, dew, due*; *main, mane, Maine*; *vain, vane, vein*; and *gnu, knew, new* (see game cards, page 23, for *knew* and *new*).

※ **Synonym or Antonym Concentration:** Use synonyms or antonyms in place of homophones.

ate	eye
eight	I
dear	for
deer	four

Vocabulary-Building Card Games: Grade 2 © 2008 by Liane B. Onish, Scholastic Teaching Resources

hear	knew
here	new
hour	made
our	maid

tail	some
tale	sum
sew	son
so	sun

Vocabulary-Building Card Games: Grade 2 © 2008 by Liane B. Onish, Scholastic Teaching Resources

Golly, Gee! Circus Cats!

Skill: Sorting vocabulary words by initial consonant sounds (hard and soft *c* and *g*)

Number of Players: 2, or teams of 8

Object of the Game: To sort vocabulary words beginning with *c* and *g* by initial sounds

Play outdoors or in an open space

How to Play

Two Players:

1. Mix up the cards and place facedown in front of each player.

2. Players turn over one card at a time, read the word, and then place the card in the correct container.

3. The winner is the first player to correctly sort all the word cards.

Teams:

1. Shuffle first. Place a stack of cards facedown in front of each team. Place the labeled containers inside the rings on the floor.

2. The first player on each team takes the top card, reads the word, and then runs to the circus ring for that initial sound, and places the card inside the container. That player runs back to the team and the next player repeats the procedure.

3. The winner is the first team to correctly sort all the word cards.

More Ways to Play

※ **Center Setup:** Place word cards and sorting containers at a center area. Let children visit individually or with partners to sort the cards by consonant sound. Provide blank game card templates (page 72) and invite children to add new words to the game.

※ **Calling All Cats:** Make four signs by enlarging and gluing each picture card to a sheet of tagboard. Display each sign in a corner of the classroom. Give each child a word card. (Use the blank game card templates on page 72 to create additional cards as needed.) Have children read their card and go to the corresponding area of the classroom. As children gather, encourage them to share their cards with one another to review the initial consonant sounds.

Materials

※ game cards (pages 26–28)

※ round containers

※ tape

※ index cards (in two colors)

※ glue

※ yarn

Getting Ready

Photocopy and cut apart the game cards. Tape each picture card to a container. Photocopy and cut apart a set of word cards for each player or team. Glue word cards to index cards, using a different color for each set. To make circus rings (for team play), use yarn to make four large circles on the floor (or use hula hoops). Place a container inside each circus ring to serve as a label and to keep cards in place.

circus

guitar

cat

giraffe

cake	celery
camel	cent
cat	circus
comb	city

game

gentle

get

gerbil

goes

giant

guitar

giraffe

Vocabulary-Building Card Games: Grade 2 © 2008 by Liane B. Onish, Scholastic Teaching Resources

Big Number Battle

Skill: Reading and using ordinal number words

Number of Players: Pairs

Object of the Game: To collect all the word cards

How to Play

1. Mix up the cards and deal out all the cards facedown. Players keep their cards facedown in a pile.

2. Play as you would the card game War. Players turn over their top cards at the same time and place them in the center of the table or playing space.

3. The player whose card has the higher ordinal number takes the two cards and adds them to the bottom of his or her pile.

4. When players turn over cards with the same number, they do the following: Players each place one additional card facedown and another card faceup. The player with the higher card wins all the cards in play. If the second faceup cards are also the same, players repeat the process.

5. The winner is the player who collects all the cards.

Materials

✳ game cards (pages 30–31)

Getting Ready

Photocopy four sets of the number word cards (for 64 cards total).

More Ways to Play

✳ **Low Number Winners:** Follow the same directions, but with the lower number card winning the round.

✳ **Beat the Clock:** Set a timer for 15 minutes. When the bell rings, the player with the most cards is the winner.

✳ **Numeral Card Twist:** Create a new deck using ordinal number word cards and adding numeral cards. Players win the round by either having a numeral or number word card that is higher.

first	fifth
second	sixth
third	seventh
fourth	eighth

Vocabulary-Building Card Games: Grade 2 © 2008 by Liane B. Onish, Scholastic Teaching Resources

Vocabulary-Building Card Games: Grade 2 © 2008 by Liane B. Onish, Scholastic Teaching Resources

ninth	thirteenth
tenth	fourteenth
eleventh	fifteenth
twelfth	sixteenth

ABC Order Races

Skill: Alphabetizing

Number of Players: 1 or 2, or teams

Object of the Game: To arrange vocabulary words in alphabetical order

Materials

* word cards (ten or more) for words with consecutive initial letters (choose any from the book, or use the blank word card templates, page 72, to create your own)
* timer
* glue
* index cards
* tables or whiteboard trays (for teams)

Getting Ready

Photocopy and cut apart the word cards. Glue each set of word cards to index cards. Use a different color for each set. For two players or teams, make two sets of word cards.

How to Play

One Player:

1. Mix up a set of word cards. Set the timer for one minute.
2. The player arranges the cards in alphabetical order.
3. At the end of one minute, the player counts the number of cards in correct alphabetical order.

Two Players:

1. Mix up a set of cards for each player.
2. Players place their cards in alphabetical order.
3. The winner is the first player to alphabetize the word cards.

Teams:

1. Mix up each set of cards. Teams line up some distance from their playing field (table or whiteboard tray). Stack a set of cards facedown in front of each team.
2. The first runner takes the top card and runs to the playing field. The player places the card about where it should go in alphabetical order. For example, the card *all* would be placed on the far left of the playing field, the card *worry* on the far right. After placing the card on the playing field, the player runs to the back of the line.
3. Each team player adds one card to the playing field and rearranges the cards that are there as needed to maintain alphabetical order.
4. The winner is the first team to correctly alphabetize the set of word cards.

More Ways to Play

* **Random ABC Order:** Choose ten or more non-consecutive vocabulary words to alphabetize.
* **Get, Giggle, Goofy:** For a challenge, choose word cards that require children to alphabetize to the second (or third) letter.

Word Mix-Up

How to Play

1. Explain that anagrams are words formed by rearranging the letters of another word. Write the word *art* on the chalkboard. Ask children to use the letters *a*, *r*, and *t* to make a word that names an animal (*rat*). Explain that *art* and *rat* are anagrams.

2. Give each player or pair an envelope. Players look at the pictures on their envelope and use the letter cards to spell the words that name the pictures.

3. Players exchange envelopes and play again.

More Ways to Play

* **More Anagrams:** Make letter cards, and picture cards when possible, for the following anagrams: *earth-heart, fast-fats, flow-wolf, ours-sour, pins-spin, slip-lips, sink-skin, won-now.* For words that are difficult to picture, such as *flow, ours,* and *now,* you might invite students to draw pictures. Discuss their drawings as a class before using them in the game.

* **Cloze Context:** Have students work in pairs to write cloze context sentences for anagrams. Use their sentences in place of picture cards.

* **Mystery Anagrams:** Use the letter cards without the picture cards to create mystery anagrams. Place each set of letter cards in an envelope. Challenge children to arrange the letters to spell two words.

Materials

* game cards (page 34)
* envelopes
* glue

Getting Ready

Photocopy and cut apart the game cards (pictures and letters). Glue each picture card to an envelope. Place each set of letter cards (a/r/m; s/t/o/p; b/e/a/k; r/i/n/g) in the corresponding envelope. (Make duplicate envelope setups as needed to accommodate all players.)

Vocabulary-Building Card Games: Grade 2
© 2008 by Liane B. Onish, Scholastic Teaching Resources

Mixed-Up Color-by-Number

Skill: Reading color words

Number of Players: Any number

Object of the Game: To color the numbered spaces in the picture using numbered colors

How to Play

1. Players mix up the word and pattern cards and place them facedown, and then number the backs of the cards from 1 to 16.

2. Players take turns turning over one card at a time and coloring the matching numbered space(s) on the picture according to the color word on the card. If a player turns over a pattern card (dots, swirls, wavy, zigzag), that player selects another card (if this card is also a pattern card, the player turns it over and chooses another) and then colors the matching spaces on the picture accordingly. For example, if a player selects the cards for *wavy* and *turquoise*, he or she colors turquoise wavy lines on the spaces that match the numbers on those cards.

3. When players have turned over each card and completed their pictures, they can share and compare their mixed-up art.

More Ways to Play

* **More Mixed-Up Color-by-Number:** Make more practice pages by adding numbers to pictures from coloring books.

* **A World of Colors:** Make new color word cards—for example, *cayenne, moss, chartreuse, honey, pumpkin, navy, charcoal,* and *azure.* Use the blank game card templates (page 72) to add new pattern cards—for example, bubbles, X's, stars, and stripes.

Materials

* Mixed-Up Color-by-Number picture (page 36)

* game cards (pages 37–38)

* crayons (in colors that approximate the word cards)

Getting Ready

Photocopy and cut apart one color-by-number picture and one set of 16 word and pattern cards for each player.

Teaching Tip

Children may not have crayons labeled with the exact colors indicated on the game cards, but can approximate the colors based on the meaning of the words. For example, they can use black for ebony, or purplish-red for ruby.

Mixed-Up Color-by-Number

Vocabulary-Building Card Games: Grade 2 © 2008 by Liane B. Onish, Scholastic Teaching Resources

beige	lime
chocolate	magenta
ebony	olive
lavender	peach

ruby

dots

• • • • •

teal

swirls

turquoise

wavy

violet

zigzag

Vocabulary-Building Card Games: Grade 2 © 2008 by Liane B. Onish, Scholastic Teaching Resources

Category Slap-Down

> **Skill:** Making associations among vocabulary words
>
> **Number of Players:** 4 to 6
>
> **Object of the Game:** To collect four word cards in the same category

How to Play

1. Mix up and deal all the cards.

2. Players keep their hand hidden from the others, and select a card they do not want (with the object of the game being to collect all four cards in a category).

3. Each player places an unwanted card facedown on the table. When all have an unwanted card ready, they slide it at the same time to the player to their left. Players look at their new cards and select an unwanted card to pass as before.

4. The winner is the first player to collect four cards that belong to the same category and slap the hand down on the table.

5. Other players check the winning hand to see that the four words belong to the same category.

6. Players can mix up the cards and play again.

More Ways to Play

❋ **Add a Category:** To add players, add categories. Use the blank game card templates (page 72) to make four cards for each new category. Create a new category for each additional player. Sample category sets include:

> SPACE: planet, moon, meteor, star
>
> REPTILES: alligator, tortoise, lizard, rattlesnake
>
> CAREERS: carpenter, musician, scientist, teacher
>
> TOOLS: chisel, hammer, knife, wrench
>
> FRUITS: cantaloupe, watermelon, strawberry, tangerine

Materials

❋ game cards (pages 40–42)

❋ index cards

❋ glue

Getting Ready

Photocopy and cut apart the game cards. (The game cards include six sets of category cards, with four cards per set.) Glue each game card to an index card. Put together a deck by choosing one set of four category cards for each player—for example, for four players, you might include card sets for birds, places, plants, and sea animals.

Teaching Tip

Making connections among words, such as those that belong to the same category, makes it easier for children to learn new words and broaden their vocabulary.

ostrich	arena
pigeon	school
robin	store
turkey	theater

Vocabulary-Building Card Games: Grade 2 © 2008 by Liane B. Onish, Scholastic Teaching Resources

Vocabulary-Building Card Games: Grade 2 © 2008 by Liane B. Onish, Scholastic Teaching Resources

blossom	dolphin
shrub	lobster
tree	octopus
weed	shark

evening	carrot
midnight	lettuce
morning	spinach
noon	tomato

Vocabulary-Building Card Games: Grade 2 © 2008 by Liane B. Onish, Scholastic Teaching Resources

Voca-Bees

Skill: Using vocabulary words in context

Number of Players: Whole class

Object of the Game: To win game cards by correctly using words in sentences

How to Play

1. Shuffle the cards and stack them facedown.

2. Players form two teams.

3. Read the top word for team 1. The first player on team 1 repeats the word and uses it in a sentence. If the player is correct, the player gets the Bee Card. If the player is not correct, the first player on team 2 attempts the same word. If the player on team 2 is correct, he or she keeps the card.

4. Repeat with the next word for team 2.

5. Continue as above until all players on both teams have played. The winner is the team that collects the most cards.

Materials

❊ Bee Card templates (page 72)

Getting Ready

Photocopy and cut apart the Bee Card templates. Write a word on each card. Make at least one game card per player.

More Ways to Play

❊ **Define-a-Bees:** Make a set of definition cards to go with the word cards. Give each team a set of word cards. Read a definition for team 1. Players work together to find the matching word. If they are correct, they take the definition. If not, team 2 can identify the correct word. Play continues in this way until all definitions have been matched to a word.

❊ **Spell-a-Bee:** Play as above, but have players spell the words before using them in a sentence.

Hat Tricks

Skill: Identifying parts of speech

Number of Players: Individuals or pairs

Object of the Game: To sort word cards into four categories: nouns, pronouns, verbs, and adjectives and adverbs

Materials

* game cards (pages 45–47)
* index cards
* glue
* timer (optional)

Getting Ready

Photocopy and cut apart the game cards, including four hat cards and a set of 16 word cards for each player or pair. Label the hat cards "Nouns," "Pronouns," "Verbs," and "Adjectives and Adverbs," and then glue each to a shoe box or bag. Glue the word cards to index cards, using a different color for each set.

How to Play

1. Read the words with players and have them tell which category each word belongs to: nouns, pronouns, verbs, or adjectives and adverbs. (Review terminology first and provide examples.)

2. Mix up a set of cards for each player. Place the boxes nearby.

3. Set the timer for three minutes.

4. Players sort the words by category, placing the cards in the correct boxes.

5. For more than one player, the winner is the player with the most cards in the correct "hats" at the end of three minutes.

> ## More Ways to Play

* **Team Players:** Mix up a set of cards for each team and stack them facedown at one end of a playing area. Place a set of labeled hat boxes at the opposite end. Have teams line up behind their cards. The first player on each team takes the top card, runs to the other end, and places the card in the correct hat. Then the player runs to the back of the line and the next player goes. The first team to sort all cards correctly wins.

* **More Sorting Hats:** Add other hats and word cards for proper nouns, plural nouns, and past-tense verbs.

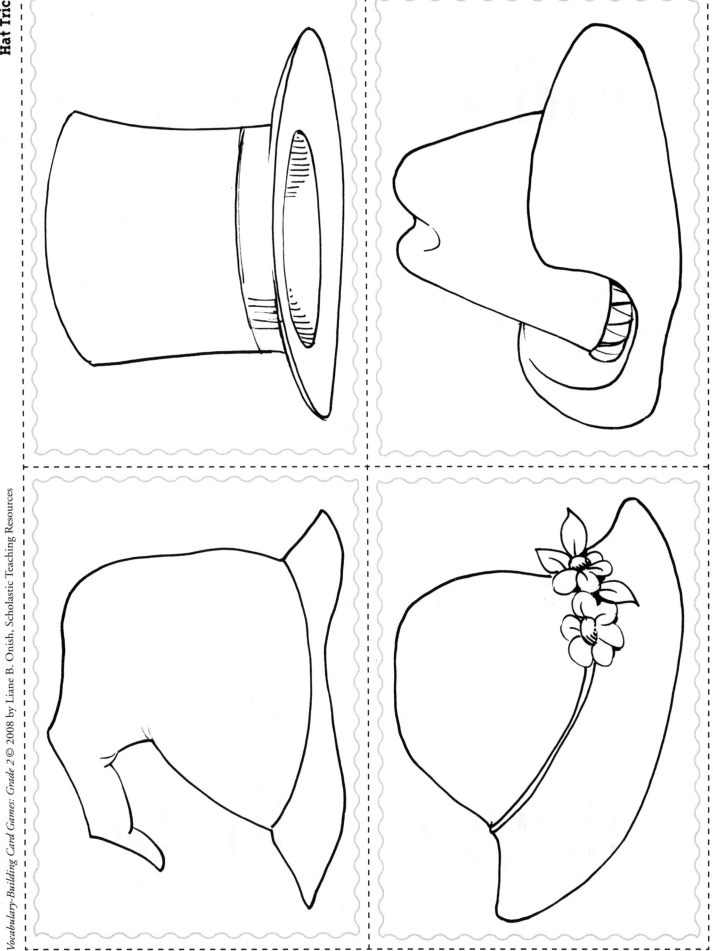

bridge	he
country	I
month	she
village	them

Vocabulary-Building Card Games: Grade 2 © 2008 by Liane B. Onish, Scholastic Teaching Resources

Vocabulary-Building Card Games: Grade 2 © 2008 by Liane B. Onish, Scholastic Teaching Resources

buy

always

cook

colorful

help

early

pull

under

Fishing for Opposites

Skill: Reading and matching opposites

Number of Players: 2 or 3

Object of the Game: To get rid of one's cards by finding pairs of antonyms

Materials

❋ game cards (pages 49–51)

❋ index cards

❋ glue

Getting Ready

Photocopy and cut apart a set of game cards for each group of players. Glue each card to an index card. You may also use the blank game card templates (page 72) to add new pairs of antonyms to the deck.

How to Play

1. Mix up the cards and deal seven cards each if two players and five cards each if three players. Spread out the remaining cards facedown in the center of the table. This is the "fish pond."

2. Players look at their cards and remove any cards that are opposites—for example: *all* and *none*. Players place each pair of cards facedown in front of them.

3. Play continues as for Go Fish. The first player is the one sitting to the dealer's left. The first player asks the player to his or her left for a specific word that would make a pair of antonyms with a card in the player's hand. If the asked player has the card, he or she must give it to the first player. The first player then asks any other player for another card. The first player's turn continues until the asked player does not have the requested card and says, "Go fish." The player takes a card from the fish pond to end his or her turn.

4. The player who said "Go fish" asks the player to his or her left for a card.

5. Play continues until one player has found the antonym match for all his or her cards. If two players finish at the same time, the player with the most pairs wins (or if both have the same number, these players tie).

More Ways to Play

❋ **Concentration:** Shuffle the cards and place them facedown in an array. (Reduce the number of cards for a simpler version, removing pairs of matching cards.) Players play as they would play Concentration, turning over two cards at a time to make an antonym match.

❋ **Find Your Opposite:** Give each child a word card. Make extra cards as needed so that each child has a card and can make an antonym match with another child. Have children move about the room, looking for their opposite. When children find their partners, they sit down and read their words together. As a variation, time children. Record the time it takes for all children to pair up by antonym. Play again with the same words and challenge children to beat their first time.

Vocabulary-Building Card Games: Grade 2 © 2008 by Liane B. Onish, Scholastic Teaching Resources

after

before

all

better

worse

close

open

few

many

goodbye

hello

large

small

left

right

Vocabulary-Building Card Games: Grade 2 © 2008 by Liane B. Onish, Scholastic Teaching Resources

Vocabulary-Building Card Games: Grade 2 © 2008 by Liane B. Onish, Scholastic Teaching Resources

less	more
loud	quiet
narrow	wide
start	stop

Face It

Skill: Illustrating words for emotions

Number of Players: 2 or more

Object of the Game: To match faces with words for feelings

Materials

❋ game cards (pages 53–54)

❋ drawing materials

Getting Ready

Photocopy and cut apart two sets of picture cards and one set of word cards for each player. (Each player will have a set of eight "face" cards and eight word cards.)

How to Play

1. Players look at their word cards, then draw features on each face and fill in the speech bubbles as desired, to match a "feelings" word. Players illustrate a different word on each face.

2. Players place the matching word card facedown next to each face.

3. Children rotate to each player's cards, looking at the faces, guessing the words, and turning over the word cards to check their answers. Players then turn the word cards facedown and move on to a new set of cards (if more than two players).

More Ways to Play

❋ **Make More Faces:** Make additional faces available to players who want to complete faces for expressions of their own choosing.

❋ **Face Readers:** Enlarge and photocopy the speech and thought balloons (below). Tack them up on a bulletin board next to pictures of expressive faces cut from magazines. Have children fill in the speech and thought balloons to tell what they think the people might be saying or thinking.

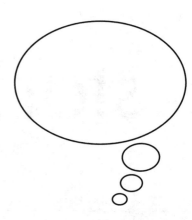

anger

scream

fear

surprise

giggle

weep

goofy

worry

Vocabulary-Building Card Games: Grade 2 © 2008 by Liane B. Onish, Scholastic Teaching Resources

Transportation Mix-Up

Skill: Matching words and pictures

Number of Players: 4 to 8

Object of the Game: To find words and matching picture cards to complete the train

How to Play

1. Mix up the picture cards. Place word cards along a whiteboard tray.

2. Each player takes a train engine and car and lines them up. Distribute picture cards evenly to players (one or more to each, facedown).

3. When you say "All aboard!," players turn over a picture card and then find the matching word card on the whiteboard tray.

4. Players place the matching picture and word card in the car, add another train car to their train, and turn over a new picture card and repeat.

5. Play continues until players' trains are four or more cars long.

6. To play again, collect the cards and mix up each set (picture and word). Redistribute picture cards, and place word cards in the whiteboard tray.

More Ways to Play

✳ **Big Trains:** Brainstorm other means of transportation with children. Have them find pictures in magazines or draw the vehicles to make additional picture cards. Help them spell the words for the matching word cards. Provide additional copies of the train cars and let children add on.

✳ **A to Z Trains:** As children collect picture and word card matches, have them arrange the words on the train in alphabetical order. (This may mean moving cars around as they add new sets of cards or cars to the train.) Use words such as *ambulance* and *automobile* to teach alphabetizing to the second letter.

✳ **Train Car Sort:** Provide children with multiple train engines and cars. Have children set up several trains and then sort matching words and pictures onto the trains. Model sorting: Show children the unicycle, bicycle, and subway. Have them tell which one does not belong and why. (They might say, for example, that a subway is for many people; a unicycle and bicycle are for one.) Encourage children to tell the sorting rule for each train—for example, an ambulance and fire engine might go together on one train because they are emergency vehicles.

Materials

✳ train templates (engine and cars; page 56)

✳ game cards (pages 57–58)

Getting Ready

Photocopy and cut out one train engine and at least four cars per player. (Players will need one train car for each picture-word match they make.) Photocopy and cut apart a set of picture and word cards. (You can make multiple copies of each, so that more than one player can match each word and picture. Or use the blank game card templates on page 72 to create additional picture and word card sets. See Big Trains, left.)

Transportation Mix-Up

Vocabulary-Building Card Games: Grade 2 © 2008 by Liane B. Onish, Scholastic Teaching Resource

ambulance

automobile

bicycle

fire engine

monorail

subway

tractor

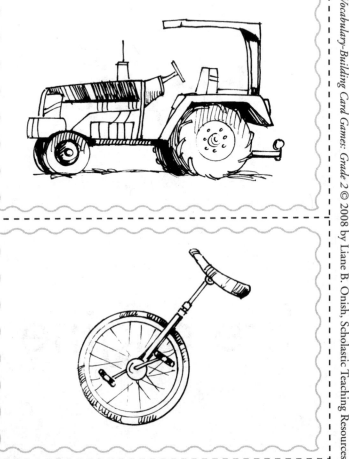

unicycle

Vocabulary-Building Card Games: Grade 2 © 2008 by Liane B. Onish, Scholastic Teaching Resources

Now and Then

Skill: Matching present with irregular past tense

Number of Players: Up to 24

Object of the Game: To match present and past tenses of irregular verbs

Play outdoors or in an open space

How to Play

Version 1:

1. Post "Now" and "Then" signs at either end of an open area.

2. Discuss present- and past-tense verbs by asking children to name words that tell about something happening now and something that happened in the past—for example, "We sing songs in our classroom" (*sing*) and "This morning we sang a new song" (*sang*).

3. Give one card, facedown, to each player. When you say "Go!," players read their words and run to the "Now" area if their word is present tense or the "Then" area for a past-tense verb.

Version 2:

1. Discuss present and past tense as above.

2. Give one card, facedown, to each player. (Make sure each player can make a match with another player.) When you say "Go!" start the timer. Players find the classmate who has the past or present tense of the word on their card, and then sit together and read their words and use them in a sentence.

3. When all players have found their partners, stop the clock. Record the date and time. Play later in the week and compare times.

More Ways to Play

❄ **New Words to Know:** Encourage children to be on the lookout in their reading for past-tense forms of irregular verbs. Provide blank game card templates (page 72) for them to record their words. Make cards with the matching present-tense verbs. Use the cards to make new versions of the game.

❄ **Three-Way Sort:** Create sets of game cards for past-tense verbs that are formed by adding *-ed* (*jumped*) and by doubling the final consonant and adding *-ed* (*skipped*). Set up a three-column chart (labeled with words that represent each way of forming past tense). Have children sort the words, reading the words and using them in a sentence.

Materials

❄ game cards (pages 60–62)

❄ 2 sheets of tagboard

❄ marker

❄ timer

Getting Ready

There are two versions of this game. For each version, photocopy and cut apart a set of word cards. (Use the blank game card templates on page 72 to make additional word cards as needed, so that there is a word card for each player. Add game cards in pairs of present and past tenses.) For version 1, use tagboard to make two large signs that read "Now" and "Then."

blow	blew
catch	caught
come	came
drink	drank

Vocabulary-Building Card Games: Grade 2 © 2008 by Liane B. Onish, Scholastic Teaching Resources

keep

kept

lend

lent

say

said

sing

sang

sleep

slept

sting

stung

take

took

write

wrote

Vocabulary-Building Card Games: Grade 2 © 2008 by Liane B. Onish, Scholastic Teaching Resources

Picture This

Skill: Recognizing multiple-meaning words (homophones)

Number of Players: Any number

Object of the Game: To illustrate words with multiple meanings

How to Play

1. Discuss multiple-meaning words. Use the word *tie* as an example. Have players watch you tie a knot in a piece of string. Then ask: "What is it called when two people run a race and finish at the same time?" (*a tie*) Explain that many words have more than one meaning.

2. Distribute word strips and drawing materials. Players draw a picture to illustrate one meaning of the word on the card. Make dictionaries available.

3. Have players cut their cards into two pieces, separating the word and the picture. Collect word and picture cards.

4. Mix up the picture cards and place along a whiteboard tray or on a table. Distribute word cards.

5. When you say "Go," players find a picture that goes with the word on the card.

6. Players return to their seats when they have a picture and word card pair. Have players take turns telling the meaning of their word, as represented by the picture. Discuss other meanings of each word.

More Ways to Play

* **Two-Part Pictures:** Use sentence strips (or strips of tagboard or white drawing paper) to make three-part strips. Give each player a word card. Have players illustrate two meanings of their word—for example, for the word *bat*, a player might draw a baseball bat and the animal. Then play as above, cutting the strips into three parts, arranging all pictures in random order on the whiteboard tray or the table. Shuffle the word cards and give one to each player. Have players find two matching pictures for their words.

* **More Picture This:** Use content area words as a game focus. Have children illustrate the vocabulary words and then continue as above in steps 3–6.

Materials

* word strips (page 64)
* drawing materials
* dictionaries

Getting Ready

Photocopy and cut apart a word strip for each player. Write each of the following words on a strip in the space provided (on the left side): *ball, bark, bat, cap, drop, fall, fan, line, pen, spot, story, yard*. Use other words to create additional strips as needed, choosing words that represent picturable items. For a list of "picture words," see *Phonics From A to Z* by Wiley Blevins (Scholastic, 2006).

Teaching Tip

To add a challenge, start a timer when you say "Go." Stop the timer when all players have found a picture. Record the time. Collect the cards, redistribute, and play again. Compare times.

Vocabulary-Building Card Games: Grade 2 © 2008 by Liane B. Onish, Scholastic Teaching Resources

Bits and Pieces

Skill: Using syllables to make words

Number of Players: Pairs

Object of the Game: To find the syllables of the words that match the pictures

How to Play

1. To model the game, mix up the syllable cards *pen, cil, ta,* and *ble.* Read each syllable card as you place it on a whiteboard tray. Explain that syllables are word parts. Then hold up a pencil and have children find the syllables that, together, make the word *pencil.* Reshuffle the cards, then read them again as you place them on the whiteboard tray. Repeat with the syllables for *table,* pointing to a table as children find the syllables that make the word.

2. Give each pair of players an envelope of syllable cards. Place a picture card facedown in front of each pair.

3. When you say "Go," players turn over the picture card and race to find the syllables that make the word that names the picture. When players find the correct syllable cards, they stand and hold up the cards in order to spell the word—for example, *tur/tle.*

4. The winner is the first pair standing with the correct syllable cards in order.

More Ways to Play

❋ **Independent Bits and Pieces:** Place all picture and syllable cards in an envelope. Include writing materials. Players find the syllables that spell the name for each picture and record them on a sheet of paper; they can use a different color to highlight each syllable.

❋ **Syllable Circle:** Gather players in a circle and give each a picture card. Have players say aloud the name for their picture. Place all syllable cards in a bag and place the bag in the center. Have the first player select a card. If the syllable is part of the word that names the player's picture, the player keeps it. If not, the player places the card faceup on the floor next to the bag. Play continues in this way, with players either selecting a card from the bag or any card from the floor, and attempting to build the word that names their picture.

Materials

❋ index cards (to make syllable cards)

❋ game cards (page 66)

❋ envelopes

Getting Ready

On index cards, write the following syllables (one per card): *ban, jo, chick, en, e, qual, fin, ger, hang, er, pock, et, slip, per, tur, tle.* Make a set of syllable cards for each pair of players. Place each set of cards in an envelope. Photocopy and cut apart the picture cards, making one card for each pair of players. Make an extra set of syllable cards to model how to play: *pen, cil, ta, ble.*

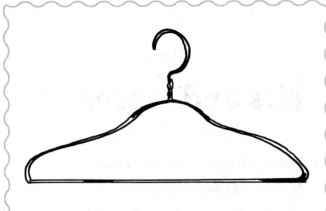

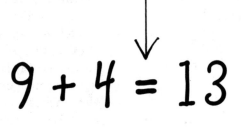

$$9 + 4 = 13$$

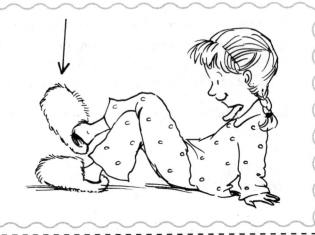

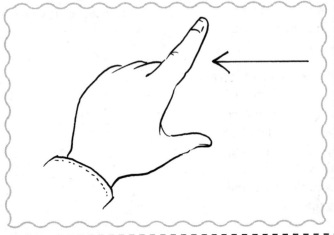

Vocabulary-Building Card Games: Grade 2 © 2008 by Liane B. Onish, Scholastic Teaching Resources

Word-O!

Skill: Writing and reading vocabulary words

Number of Players: Individuals, pairs, small groups, or whole class

Object of the Game: To get three words in a row, down, across, or diagonally

How to Play

1. Read each word aloud. Players write the word in any space on their game board. Players may choose any 9 of the 12 words.

2. When all players have 9 words written on their game boards, shuffle the 12 word cards and stack them facedown.

3. Play as you would Bingo. The caller reads the word on the top card. If players find the word on their game board, they place a marker on it.

4. Continue reading the top card and setting it aside until one player has three words in a row and says, "Word-O!"

More Ways to Play

✻ **Defining Bingo:** Select 12 word cards and have players fill in their game boards with any 9. The caller gives a definition for each word, but does not say the word. Players mark the words on their boards that go with each definition.

✻ **Bigger Bingo:** Make 4 x 4 game boards. Vary how to win: four corners, four in a row vertically or horizontally only, two and two forming a square, seven forming an L.

Materials

✻ game board (page 68)

✻ word cards

✻ small markers for each player (such as paper clips or buttons)

Getting Ready

Photocopy a Word-O! game board for each player. Distribute game boards and markers to all players. Select, photocopy, and cut apart any 12 word cards. Or use the blank game card templates (page 72) to create game cards using any vocabulary you wish.

Word-O!

Vocabulary-Building Card Games: Grade 2 © 2008 by Liane B. Onish, Scholastic Teaching Resources

What Went Where?

Skill: Recognizing words that begin with *w* and *wh*

Number of Players: Small groups

Object of the Game: To practice reading words that begin with *w* and *wh* and to find the missing word

How to Play

1. Give players 30 seconds to study the words.

2. Players put their heads down or turn their backs and close their eyes while you remove one word. Rearrange the remaining words (optional).

3. The winner is the first player to identify the missing word and use it in a sentence.

4. Repeat to provide practice with each word.

More Ways to Play

* **More to Remember, Faster, Too:** To make the game more challenging, increase the number of words (use the blank game card templates on page 72 to add words), reduce the study time, or both.

* **Know and No:** Use the game as a model for providing practice with words that begin with *kn* and *n*, such as *know, knew, knee, knot, knit, no, new, not, note,* and *noise.* As with the original game, notice opportunities to teach homophones, such as *know* and *no.*

Materials

* game cards (pages 70–71)
* thumbtacks
* timer (optional)

Getting Ready

Photocopy and cut apart the word cards. Tack six or more cards to a bulletin board (or spread out on a table in a 2 x 3 array).

Teaching Tip

Use the game as an opportunity to teach homophones (words that sound the same but have different spellings and meanings), using words such as *where* and *wear* as examples. Encourage children to think about meaning and spelling when they read these words or use them in their writing.

wear	woman
week	women
welcome	wonder
went	wool

Vocabulary-Building Card Games: Grade 2 © 2008 by Liane B. Onish, Scholastic Teaching Resources

Vocabulary-Building Card Games: Grade 2 © 2008 by Liane B. Onish, Scholastic Teaching Resources

whale	which
what	while
when	white
where	why

Wild
Card

Wild
Card

any

brown

ask

but

best

candle

both

child

Vocabulary-Building Card Games: Grade 2 © 2008 by Liane B. Onish, Scholastic Teaching Resources

children

dinosaur

cold

doctor

crawl

dresser

desk

end

Vocabulary-Building Card Games: Grade 2 © 2008 by Liane B. Onish, Scholastic Teaching Resources

every

gift

fence

hers

follow

him

funny

house

how

now

into

once

just

pair

know

party

Vocabulary-Building Card Games: Grade 2 © 2008 by Liane B. Onish, Scholastic Teaching Resources

Vocabulary-Building Card Games: Grade 2 © 2008 by Liane B. Onish, Scholastic Teaching Resources

please	puzzle
police	quiz
pretty	read
purple	remember

sandwich

soon

short

sound

should

street

snake

sure

Vocabulary-Building Card Games: Grade 2 © 2008 by Liane B. Onish, Scholastic Teaching Resources

teacher

thermos

thank

tower

their

town

then

twin

Vocabulary-Building Card Games: Grade 2 © 2008 by Liane B. Onish, Scholastic Teaching Resources

upset

wheelchair

us

would

volcano

year

wait

zip

Vocabulary-Building Card Games: Grade 2 © 2008 by Liane B. Onish, Scholastic Teaching Resources